W9-AYP-114

SEASONS
A Gwendolyn Brooks Experience

SEASONS
A Gwendolyn Brooks Experience

EDITED BY

Nora Brooks Blakely   *Cynthia A. Walls*

ILLUSTRATIONS BY

Jan Spivey Gilchrist

Brooks
PERMISSIONS

THIRD WORLD PRESS FOUNDATION

CHICAGO

Seasons
A Gwendolyn Brooks Experience

Text copyright © 2017 Nora Brooks Blakely
Illustration and design copyright © 2017 Jan Spivey Gilchrist
Edited by Nora Brooks Blakely, Cynthia A. Walls
Sketch of Gwendolyn Brooks on title page - A gift to Gwendolyn from her brother, Raymond Brooks

Published by Brooks Permissions & Third World Press Foundation • Chicago

Brooks Permissions • P.O. Box 19355 • Chicago, IL 60619
www.gwendolynbrooks.net

Library of Congress Control Number: 2016954687
Hardcover   978-0-9795803-0-7   Paperback   978-0-9795803-1-4
20 19 18 17   6 5 4 3 2 1
Gwendolyn Brooks • American Poetry (20th century) • Black Literature • African-American Poetry
Women's Literature • African-American Poets - Young Adult Literature

First Edition
Printed in the United States of America

Dedications

To Mama, and all those who are connected to her, by genes or destinations.
–NORA BROOKS BLAKELY

Dedicated to a beautiful rose: my mother, Rosie Lee Walls and the rest of her bouquet—my sister Lorrie Walls and my daughter, Tahanni Walls.
–CYNTHIA A. WALLS

Especially for the children of Chicago and to the children around the world: know that Gwendolyn Brooks lived and loved children.
–JAN SPIVEY GILCHRIST

_____A memory

Nichole L. Shields

As early as the fourth grade, a seed to become a writer was planted in my heart.

Often admitting to school chums that desire over the years, I tried my hand at writing essays, short stories, and poetry—narrative poetry in particular. Years later, I had an up close and personal encounter with Gwendolyn Brooks in the lobby of a local theater company and I shyly mentioned my desire to write.

With parental praise and glee, Ms. Brooks reached into her tote bag and out came a copy of her recently released, *Children Coming Home,* which she signed and gave to me. Needless to say, I was overwhelmed by her generosity and her interest in me, a young woman with legal pads and notebooks full of writings. Bidding me well with my literary aspirations, I marveled on that encounter for years, until the next—five years later.

This time, I'd courageously entered the open mic poetry contest at the annual Gwendolyn Brooks Conference at Chicago State University, and lo and behold, a panel of judges selected me as one of three winners, receiving a warm hug and a crisp $100.00 bill from the pocketbook of none other than Gwendolyn Brooks herself.

That hug, that pat on the back, was yet another affirmation that I, a young budding writer needed to follow my heart.

I have had the nurturing support of a wonderful mother, who has always cheered me on; a fourth grade teacher who saw something more special in me than any other student in her class; and a plethora of instructors and professors over the years whose instruction helped me to grow. My good fortune, combined with several seals of approval by Gwendolyn Brooks has led me to my lifelong desire to write, allowing me to share my work with readers all over the world. It is especially rewarding when I can share the works of my literary fairy godmother, Gwendolyn Brooks.

My contribution to this collection of carefully selected classic writings is my gift to readers, young and old, who would like a peep in the world of a writer who touched so many. This collection is meant to offer insightfulness, joy, and celebration to one of the world's most respected writers.

Enjoy *Seasons*…and may you, too, achieve your aspirations.

With much gratitude and sincerity,

Nichole L. Shields

Acknowledgements

"...we are each other's harvest"
- *Gwendolyn Brooks*

The beautiful harvests which have resulted in Seasons and the evolution of Brooks Permissions, have been made possible by so many people in so many ways. Here are a few. THANK YOU!

Haki R. Madhubuti
Nichole L. Shields
Third World Press
Poetry Foundation
Dr. Kelvin Gilchrist
Quraysh Ali Lansana
Louis Segovia
B.J. Bolden
Denise Borel
Liz Owens
Carolyn Aguila
Shannon Stiles

Broadside Press
Jan Spivey Gilchrist
Ebony Magazine
O Magazine
Barbara Turner
Chiquita Morgan
Jacqueline Bryant
D.H. Melhem
Bryant Smith
Pamela Williams
Felicia Furcron-Dixon
Donzell Gordon

Some poems were first published in *Harper's Magazine*, *Poetry* and *Voice*.

ABOUT...
Nora Brooks Blakely

Former Producing Artistic Director and primary playwright for Chocolate Chips Theatre Company in Chicago for twenty-nine years. Her readings and lectures have been conducted in several states. Ms. Blakely taught for eight years in the Chicago Public Schools and spent over twenty years teaching drama and writing workshops for students and teachers. Nora has also served on boards and committees for several youth and arts organizations. She is the daughter of two writers, Henry Blakely and Gwendolyn Brooks, and founded Brooks Permissions, a company which manages her mother's body of work and promotes its continued relevance in the 21st century and beyond.

ABOUT...
Cynthia A. Walls

Ms. Walls is the Vice President of *Brooks Permissions*. She received her B.A. with a major in Theater and Speech from DePaul University but before focusing on the arts she held several positions in finance. She also taught drama classes and workshops at numerous schools, colleges, commercial institutions and museums throughout Chicago. Cynthia held the position of Director of Operations for Chocolate Chips Theatre Company for all of its twenty-nine years. She has directed theatrical productions for over 30 years and currently is the director for Aurora Performance Group. She directs stage presentations in the South region of the Chicago Church of Christ.

Before her position with Brooks Permissions, Ms. Walls managed The David Company, a publishing firm owned by Gwendolyn Brooks. She is currently working on her forthcoming novel, *Callie Rose*.

ABOUT...
Jan Spivey Gilchrist

Jan Spivey Gilchrist illustrated, <u>The Girl Who Buried Her Dreams in a Can,</u> 2015, by Oprah's All-Time Favorite Guest, Dr. Tererai Trent. <u>The Great Migration: Journey to the North,</u> 2011, by Eloise Greenfield, won the Coretta Scott King Honor Book Award, NAACP Nomination, Junior Library Guild Award, CCBC Best Books 2012, and Georgia State Nomination. <u>Children of Long Ago,</u> Putnam, by Lessie Jones Little, 1988 won the Peoples Choice Award, <u>Nathaniel Talking,</u> 1990, by Eloise Greenfield, won her the Coretta Scott King Award for Illustration. She won the 1992 Coretta Scott King, Honor Book Award, for, <u>Night on Neighborhood Street</u>, also by Ms. Greenfield. <u>My America,</u> written and illustrated by Jan Spivey Gilchrist, along with illustrations by Ashley Bryan, won the Parent's Choice Book Award in 2007. Illustrator of over seventy-seven award-winning books. Ms. Gilchrist's books have received numerous prestigious awards. She was inducted into the prestigious Society of Illustrators, 2000.

ABOUT...

Founded in 2001, the company manages the literary works of acclaimed poet Gwendolyn Brooks. Brooks Permissions processes numerous requests for Ms. Brooks' works annually, working with mainstream, educational, and independent publishers, as well as individual artists for projects ranging from literary anthologies and academic course packs to theatrical performances, multimedia projects and more. In 2015 <u>Brooks Permissions</u> expanded to include programming and products which help to shine a well-deserved and continuing spotlight on Gwendolyn Brooks' life and work.

Third World Press Foundation provides quality literature that primarily focuses on issues, themes and critique related to an African-American public. In 2017, TWPF will celebrate its 50th anniversary.

Other Books by Gwendolyn Brooks

POETRY

A Street in Bronzeville	1945
Annie Allen	1949
Bronzeville Boys and Girls	1956
The Bean Eaters	1960
Selected Poems	1963, 2006
We Real Cool	1966
The Wall	1967
In the Mecca	1968
Riot	1969
Family Pictures	1970
Aloneness	1971
The Tiger Who Wore White Gloves	1974
Beckonings	1975
To Disembark	1981
Black Love	1982
The Near-Johannesburg Boy and Other Poems	1986
Blacks	1987
Winnie	1988
Gottschalk and the Grande Tarantelle	1988
Children Coming Home	1991
In Montgomery *and Other Poems*, (*posthumously*)	2003

Other Publications

Maud Martha	1953
The World of Gwendolyn Brooks	1971
A Broadside Treasury (*editor*)	1971
Jump Bad: A New Chicago Anthology (*editor*)	1971
Report from Part One	1972
The Tiger Who Wore White Gloves	1974
A Capsule Course in Black Poetry Writing	1975
(*with Don L. Lee, Keorapetse Kgositsile and Dudley Randall*)	
Primer for Blacks	1980
Young Poets Primer	1981
Very Young Poets	1983
Report from Part Two	1995

ABOUT...
Gwendolyn Brooks

Born in Topeka, Kansas, June 7, 1917, she was brought home to Chicago after her first few weeks of life. She married Henry L. Blakely II in 1939. They had 2 children, Henry L. Blakely III and Nora Brooks Blakely.

The first Black person to ever win the Pulitzer Prize *(1950)*, she received over seventy honorary degrees as well as many other honors and awards, including Poet Laureate of Illinois *(30+ years)*, inductee of the National Women's Hall of Fame, an Academy of American Poets Fellowship, the National Medal of Arts, National Endowment for the Humanities' Jefferson Award and Consultant in Poetry to the Library of Congress. However, Ms. Brooks did not just receive awards. She sponsored countless one-time, and on-going awards at elementary schools and high schools. She also developed awards for adult writers *(young and established)* and was well-known for her generosity and support of individual artists. Her published works include several books of poetry for adults and children, one novel, writing manuals, and two volumes of her autobiography.

Ms. Brooks taught at several colleges and universities. To date, five schools have been named after her, as well as the Illinois State Library Building and several other libraries, award programs and cultural centers.

Table of Contents

Table of Contents

Table of Contents

Foreword

Why are you reading this book?

Really? Well that's interesting. No, truly it is. But let me tell you why I think you should read it. It's about one of the greatest writers of the 20th Century. It includes her early work, her later work, poems she wrote for children and the ones she wrote for adults. Poems clear and simple sit next to cryptic works that may have you thinking for days. It's got some of her award-winning poetry as well as excerpts from her lesser known prose and essays. There's even a piece that's never been seen in print! This incredible, and important, writer is my mother, Gwendolyn Brooks. And you might be amazed at how, years later, her work still speaks to you now.

So, let me tell you a little about Mama. She was born a lonnngggg time ago in 1917. She started writing when she was 7 years old. That's right. <u>Seven</u> years old. Along with 20 books of poetry, she also wrote a novel, magazine and newspaper articles and 2 autobiographies. In addition, she edited literary collections and won all kinds of awards. She was the first Black person to <u>ever</u> win the Pulitzer Prize *(look it up!)*. She was a proud Chicagoan and proud of her heritage *(she capitalized the letter "B" in Black)*. But you can learn most of that in a class or by going online.

Here's what you don't know. Gwendolyn Brooks was a woman with a lot of loves. She loved words and the content and feel of books. She loved listening and learning. She loved children and the very idea of family. She loved the news *(even when she was horrified by it)*. But that's not all. She also loved tea and jam and fried chicken and Kleenex. She loved soap operas, socializing *(in her own way!)*, friends and music from Duke Ellington to James Brown to Monie Love. She loved trees, gray days with soft rain and giggling in early morning phone calls.

And all those loves wrapped themselves around her writing. You'll see. It's all here. There are little girls who sing, pout in their front yards, listen to frightening footfalls and delight in elegant snowfalls; boys who live in corners, die in alleys, who taste bread and butter and freedom. There are men and women who chew beans, chase challenges, struggle and sometimes surprise themselves with the laughter that still lives inside.

But why do we call this book <u>Seasons</u>, you ask? OK, even if you didn't ask I'm still going to tell you. It's because there is a time for everything.

In **Spring** we think of beginnings and youth. In this section you'll find one of my mother's earliest poems along with bright-eyed children, first love and hope.

Now, for **Summer** we've got poems of heat, powerful emotions, experiences seared into our memories from the world Outside. And, of course, things you do in the summer like going out in the yard or to the zoo.

Fall is a time of mellowing and the crack and crumble of aging. Things begin to decline, diminish, ebb… or fall apart. But as leaves fall away we see the solid structure underneath, the mature love, the plump sturdy legs of a child or the honor and strength of a hero.

Winter can be a time of cold weather, cold hearts, hard realities and death. Yet, it is also a time for quiet preparations. A time to begin again.

Learning should be all days in all ways so we offer writing lessons in **Words For All Seasons**. My mother's book, _Young Poet's Primer_ is here in it's entirety. These tips are <u>not</u> just for the young or new.

And because all the people involved in bringing this book to life believe Gwendolyn Brooks should be something more than print on paper or screen, we have done more. Images by the award-winning artist, Jan Spivey Gilchrist connect you more deeply to this acclaimed writer's work and life while memories from a small coterie of family and friends, peers and mentees help to stitch it all together.

In Mama's poem, "Aurora," she opens with the lines:

> **"We who are weak and wonderful, wicked, bewildered, wistful and wild**
> **are saying direct Good mornings through the fever."**

I believe she meant we, who are all those things, can stand strongly within the chaos of our everyday lives, willing to welcome whatever comes next.

Well! I think that's as good a place to start as any. Good Morning, fellow travelers of Worlds and Words.

Let us begin.

—Nora Brooks Blakely

Spring

This is Gwendolyn Brooks with her
brother, Raymond Brooks, in 1919

I Smile
When I See People Coming

I smile when I see people coming!
All the races of the world are
          wonder-causing.
I want to know many kinds of people.

I want the world to be like a garden.
I love not only roses,
but dandelions, daisies and tulips,
geraniums, honeysuckle, a violet,
jonquils _____
and black orchids.

To Be In Love

To be in love
Is to touch things with a lighter hand.

In yourself you stretch, you are well.

You look at things
Through his eyes.
A Cardinal is red.
A sky is blue.
Suddenly you know he knows too.
He is not there but
You know you are tasting together
The winter, or light spring weather.

His hand to take your hand is overmuch.
Too much to bear.

You cannot look in his eyes
Because your pulse must not say
What must not be said.

When he
Shuts a door—

Is not there—
Your arms are water.

And you are free
With a ghastly freedom.

You are the beautiful half
Of a golden hurt.

You remember and covet his mouth,
To touch, to whisper on.

Oh when to declare
Is certain Death!

Oh when to apprize
Is to mesmerize,

To see fall down, the Column of Gold,
Into the commonest ash.

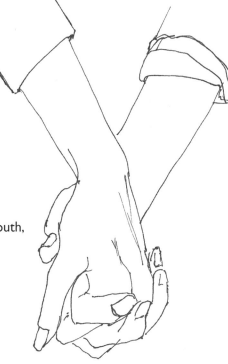

Forgive And Forget

If others neglect you,
Forget; do not sigh,
For, after all, they'll select you,
In times by and by.
If their taunts cut and hurt you,
They are sure to regret.
And, if in time, they desert you,
Forgive and forget.

The Life of Lincoln West

Ugliest little boy
that everyone ever saw.
That is what everyone said.

Even to his mother it was apparent—
when the blue-aproned nurse came into the
northeast end of the maternity ward
bearing his squeals and plump bottom
looped up in a scant receiving blanket,
bending, to pass the bundle carefully
into the waiting mother-hands—that this
was no cute little ugliness, no sly baby waywardness
that was going to inch away
as would baby fat, baby curl, and
baby spot-rash. The pendulous lip, the
branching ears, the eyes so wide and wild,
the vague unvibrant brown of the skin,
and, most disturbing, the great head.
These components of That Look bespoke
the sure fibre. The deep grain.

His father could not bear the sight of him.
His mother high-piled her pretty dyed hair and
put him among her hairpins and sweethearts,
dance slippers, torn paper roses.
He was not less than these,
he was not more.

As the little Lincoln grew,
uglily upward and out, he began
to understand that something was
wrong. His little ways of trying
to please his father, the bringing
of matches, the jumping aside at
warning sound of oh-so-large and
rushing stride, the smile that gave
and gave and gave—Unsuccessful!

Even Christmases and Easters were spoiled.
He would be sitting at the
family feasting table, really
delighting in the displays of mashed potatoes
and the rich golden
fat-crust of the ham or the festive
fowl, when he would look up and find
somebody feeling indignant about him.

What a pity what a pity. No love
for one so loving. The little Lincoln
loved Everybody. Ants. The changing
caterpillar. His much-missing mother.
His kindergarten teacher.

His kindergarten teacher—whose
concern for him was composed of one
part sympathy and two parts repulsion.
The others ran up with their little drawings.
He ran up with his.
She
tried to be as pleasant with him as
with others, but it was difficult.
For she was all pretty! all daintiness,
all tiny vanilla, with blue eyes and fluffy
sun-hair. One afternoon she
saw him in the hall looking bleak against
the wall. It was strange because the
bell had long since rung and no other
child was in sight. Pity flooded her.
She buttoned her gloves and suggested
cheerfully that she walk him home. She
started out bravely, holding him by the
hand. But she had not walked far before
she regretted it. The little monkey.
Must everyone look? And clutching her
hand like that. . . . Literally pinching
it. . . .

At seven, the little Lincoln loved
the brother and sister who
moved next door. Handsome. Well-
dressed. Charitable, often, to him. They
enjoyed him because he was
resourceful, made up
games, told stories. But when
their More Acceptable friends came they turned
their handsome backs on him. He
hated himself for his feeling
of well-being when with them despite—
Everything.

He spent much time looking at himself
in mirrors. What could be done?
But there was no
shrinking his head. There was no
binding his ears.

"Don't touch me!" cried the little
fairy-like being in the playground.

Her name was Nerissa. The many
children were playing tag, but when
he caught her, she recoiled, jerked free
and ran. It was like all the
rainbow that ever was, going off
forever, all, all the sparklings in
the sunset west.

One day, while he was yet seven,
a thing happened. In the down-town movies
with his mother a white
man in the seat beside him whispered
loudly to a companion, and pointed at
the little Linc.
"THERE! That's the kind I've been wanting
to show you! One of the best
examples of the specie. Not like
those diluted Negroes you see so much of on
the streets these days, but the
real thing.

Black, ugly, and odd. You
can see the savagery. The blunt
blankness. That is the real
thing."

His mother—her hair had never looked so
red around the dark brown
velvet of her face—jumped up,
shrieked "Go to—" She did not finish.
She yanked to his feet the little
Lincoln, who was sitting there
staring in fascination at his assessor. At the author of his
new idea.

All the way home he was happy. Of course,
he had not liked the word
"ugly."
But, after all, should he not
be used to that by now? What had
struck him, among words and meanings
he could little understand, was the phrase
"the real thing."
He didn't know quite why,
but he liked that.
He liked that very much.

When he was hurt, too much
stared at—
too much
left alone—he
thought about that. He told himself
"After all, I'm
the real thing."

It comforted him.

Young Heroes —II

To Don at Salaam

I like to see you lean back in your chair
so far you have to fall but do not—
your arms back, your fine hands
in your print pockets.

Beautiful. Impudent.
Ready for life.
A tied storm.

I like to see you wearing your boy smile
whose tribute is for two of us or three.

Sometimes in life
things seem to be moving
and they are not
and they are not
there.
You are there.

Your voice is the listened-for music.
Your act is the consolidation.

I like to see you living in the world.

home
(excerpt from Maud Martha)

WHAT had been wanted was this always, this always to last, the talking softly on this porch, with the snake plant in the jardiniere in the southwest corner, and the obstinate slip from Aunt Eppie's magnificent Michigan fern at the left side of the friendly door. Mama, Maud Martha and Helen rocked slowly in their rocking chairs, and looked at the late afternoon light on the lawn, and at the emphatic iron of the fence and at the poplar tree.

These things might soon be theirs no longer. Those shafts and pools of light, the tree, the graceful iron, might soon be viewed possessively by different eyes.

Papa was to have gone that noon, during his lunch hour, to the office of the Home Owners' Loan. If he had not succeeded in getting another extension, they would be leaving this house in which they had lived for more than fourteen years. There was little hope. The Home Owners' Loan was hard. They sat, making their plans.

"We'll be moving into a nice flat somewhere," said Mama. "Somewhere on South Park, or Michigan, or in Washington Park Court." Those flats, as the girls and Mama knew well, were burdens on wages twice the size of Papa's. This was not mentioned now.

"They're much prettier than this old house," said Helen. "I have friends I'd just as soon not bring here. And I have other friends that wouldn't come down this far for anything, unless they were in a taxi."

Yesterday, Maud Martha would have attacked her. Tomorrow she might. Today she said nothing. She merely gazed at a little hopping robin in the tree, her tree, and tried to keep the fronts of her eyes dry.

"Well, I do know," said Mama, turning her hands over and over, "that I've been getting tireder and tireder of doing that firing. From October to April, there's firing to be done."

"But lately we've been helping, Harry and I," said Maud Martha. "And sometimes in March and April and in October, and even in November, we could build a little fire in the fireplace. Sometimes the weather was just right for that."

She knew, from the way they looked at her, that this had been a mistake. They did not want to cry.

But she felt that the little line of white, somewhat ridged with smoked purple, and all that cream-shot saffron, would never drift across any western sky except that in back of this house. The rain would drum with as sweet a dullness nowhere but here. The birds on South Park were mechanical birds, no better than the poor caught canaries in those "rich" women's sun parlors.

"It's just going to kill Papa!" burst out Maud Martha. "He loves this house! He *lives* for this house!"

"He lives for us," said Helen. "It's us he loves. He wouldn't want the house, except for us."

"And he'll have us," added Mama, "wherever."

"You know, "Helen sighed, "if you want to know the truth, this is a relief. If this hadn't come up, we would have gone on, just dragged on, hanging out here forever."

"It might," allowed Mama, "be an act of God. God may just have reached down, and picked up the reins."

"Yes," Maud Martha cracked in, "that's what you always say—that God knows best."

Her mother looked at her quickly, decided the statement was not suspect, looked away.

Helen saw Papa coming. " There's Papa," said Helen.

They could not tell a thing from the way Papa was walking. It was the same dear little staccato walk, one shoulder down, then the other, then repeat, and repeat. They watched his progress. He passed the Kennedys', he passed the vacant lot, he passed Mrs. Blakemore's. They wanted to hurl themselves over the fence, into the street, and shake the truth out of his collar. He opened his gate—the gate—and still his stride and face told them nothing.

"Hello," he said.

Mama got up and followed him through the front door. The girls knew better than to go in too.

Presently Mama's head emerged. Her eyes were lamps turned on.

"It's all right," she exclaimed. "He got it. It's all over. Everything is all right."

The door slammed shut. Mama's footsteps hurried away.

"I think," said Helen, rocking rapidly, "I think I'll give a party. I haven't given a party since I was eleven. I'd like some of my friends to just casually see that we're homeowners."

a song in the front yard

I've stayed in the front yard all my life.
I want a peek at the back
Where it's rough and untended and hungry weed grows.
A girl gets sick of a rose.

I want to go in the back yard now
And maybe down the alley,
To where the charity children play.
I want a good time today.

They do some wonderful things.
They have some wonderful fun.
My mother sneers, but I say it's fine
How they don't have to go in at quarter to nine.
My mother, she tells me that Johnnie Mae
Will grow up to be a bad woman.
That George'll be taken to Jail soon or late
(On account of last winter he sold our back gate.)

But I say it's fine. Honest, I do.
And I'd like to be a bad woman, too,
And wear the brave stockings of night-black lace
And strut down the streets with paint on my face.

A Girl

There was A Girl
who set forth upon waters of life,
of living.

There were black stars set in the
blue-whites of her eyes,
before which all populace Gasped and said
"The whites of your eyes are blue."
She was gracious and grateful.
Meagerly, she nodded.

"There are enemies in the waters of Life"
it was said by those people, that populace.
"When they get you they will gut you!
Sometimes, when she heard this (one among
certain languages) Girl
would take overmuch time to shudder;
but later was fit; and again
would go on.

July 21, 1998

Jane Addams

I am Jane Addams.
I am saying to the giantless time—
to the young and yammering, to the old and corrected,
well, chiefly to children coming home
with worried faces and questions about world-survival—
"Go ahead and live your life.
You might be surprised. The world might continue."

It was not easy for <u>me</u>, in the days of the giants.
And now they call <u>me</u> a giant.
Because my capitals were Labour, Reform, Welfare,
Tenement Regulation, Juvenile Court Law (the first),
Factory Inspection, Workmen's Compensation,
Woman Suffrage, Pacifism, Immigrant Justice.
And because
Black, brown, and white and red and yellow
heavied my hand and heart.

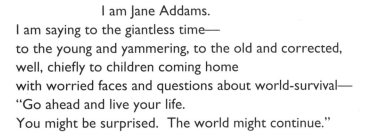

I shall tell you a thing about giants
that you do not wish to know:
Giants look in mirrors and see
almost nothing at all.
But they leave their houses nevertheless.
They lurch out of doors
to reach you, the other stretchers and strainers.
Erased under ermine or loud in tatters, oh,
moneyed or mashed, you
matter.

You matter, and giants
must bother.

I bothered.

Whatever I was tells you
the world might continue. Go on with your preparations,
moving among the quick and the dead;
nourishing here, there;
pressing a hand
among the ruins
and among the
seeds of restoration.

So speaks a giant. Jane.

Art

Art can survive
the last bugle of the last bureaucrat, can survive
the inarticulate choirs of makeiteers,
the stolid in stately places,
all flabby gallantries, all that will fall.

Lending our strength to keep art breathing we
doubly extend, refine, we clarify;
leading ourselves, (the halt, the harried) through
the icy carols and bayonets of this hour,
the divisions, vanities, the bent flowers of this hour.

We hail
what heals and sponsors and restores.

To The Young Who Want To Die

Sit down. Inhale. Exhale.
The gun will wait. The lake will wait.
The tall gall in the small seductive vial
will wait will wait:
will wait a week: will wait through April.
You do not have to die this certain day.
Death will abide, will pamper your postponement.
I assure you death will wait. Death has
a lot of time. Death can
attend to you tomorrow. Or next week. Death is
just down the street; is most obliging neighbor;
can meet you any moment.

You need not die today.
Stay here - through pout or pain or peskyness.
Stay here. See what the news is going to be tomorrow.

Graves grow no green that you can use.
Remember, green's your color. You are Spring.

SPEECH TO THE YOUNG
SPEECH TO THE PROGRESS-TOWARD

(Among them Nora and Henry III)

Say to them,
say to the down-keepers,
the sun-slappers,
the self-soilers,
the harmony-hushers,
"Even if you are not ready for day
it cannot always be night."
You will be right.
For that is the hard home-run.

Live not for battles won.
Live not for the-end-of-the-song.
Live in the along.

The Womanhood (II)

Life for my child is simple, and is good.
He knows his wish. Yes, but that is not all.
Because I know mine too.
And we both want joy of undeep and unabiding things,
Like kicking over a chair or throwing blocks out of a
      window

Or tipping over an ice box pan
Or snatching down curtains or fingering an electric outlet
Or a journey or a friend or an illegal kiss.
No. There is more to it than that.
It is that he has never been afraid.
Rather, he reaches out and lo the chair falls with a beautiful crash,
And the blocks fall, down on the people's heads,
And the water comes slooshing sloppily out across the floor.
And so forth.
Not that success, for him, is sure, infallible.
But never has he been afraid to reach.
His lesions are legion.
But reaching is his rule.

Summer

Gwendolyn Brooks Blakely and her husband *(Henry Blakely II)* at Easter in 1940. And since Henry Blakely Jr. was born in October of 1940 he's there, too *(in a way)*.

When Handed A Lemon, Make Lemonade

(title by Anonymous)

I've lived through lemons,
sugaring them.
"When handed a lemon,
make lemonade."
That is what
some sage has said.
"When handed a lemon,
make lemonade."

There is always a use
For lemon juice.

Do you know what to do with
trouble, children?
Make lemonade. Make lemonade.
"Handed a lemon, make lemonade."
"

The Chicago Defender *Sends a Man to Little Rock*

_____Fall, 1957

In Little Rock the people bear
Babes, and comb and part their hair
And watch the want ads, put repair
To roof and latch. While wheat toast burns
A woman waters multiferns.

Time upholds or overturns
The many, tight, and small concerns.

In Little Rock the people sing
Sunday hymns like anything,
Through Sunday pomp and polishing.

And after testament and tunes,
Some soften Sunday afternoons
With lemon tea and Lorna Doones.

I forecast
And I believe
Come Christmas Little Rock will cleave
To Christmas tree and trifle, weave,
From laugh and tinsel, texture fast.

In Little Rock is baseball; Barcarolle.
That hotness in July . . . the uniformed figures raw and
    implacable
And not intellectual,
Batting the hotness or clawing the suffering dust.
The Open Air Concert, on the special twilight green . . .
When Beethoven is brutal or whispers to lady-like air.
Blanket-sitters are solemn, as Johann troubles to lean
To tell them what to mean . . .

There is love, too, in Little Rock. Soft women softly
Opening themselves in kindness,
Or, pitying one's blindness,
Awaiting one's pleasure
In azure
Glory with anguished rose at the root. . . .
To wash away old semi-discomfitures.
They re-teach purple and unsullen blue.
The wispy soils go. And uncertain
Half-havings have they clarified to sures.

In Little Rock they know
Not answering the telephone is a way of rejecting life,
That it is our business to be bothered, is our business
To cherish bores or boredom, be polite
To lies and love and many-faceted fuzziness.

I scratch my head, massage the hate-I-had.
I blink across my prim and pencilled pad.
The saga I was sent for is not down.
Because there is a puzzle in this town.
The biggest News I do not dare
Telegraph to the Editor's chair:
"They are like people everywhere."

The angry Editor would reply
In hundred harryings of Why.

And true, they are hurling spittle, rock,
Garbage and fruit in Little Rock.
And I saw coiling storm a-writhe
On bright madonnas. And a scythe
Of men harassing brownish girls.
(The bows and barrettes in the curls
And braids declined away from joy.)

I saw a bleeding brownish boy. . . .

The lariat lynch-wish I deplored.

The loveliest lynchee was our Lord.

OLD WOMAN RAP

Peg

Things are different now.
I'm not strong.
I don't <u>wanna</u> go out in the yard
To see what's wrong.

I don't <u>wanna</u> mow grass,
For the sun to scorch.
I don't <u>wanna</u> govern the gutter
Nor paint the porch.

I just wanna curl myself into
a little-old-woman ball.
Or smile to myself, or eat cherries or catfish
In a clean room away down a hall.

7/15/90

38

OLD

One of the truths I know is that the oldest person is just as alive as the youngest. That sounds simple but it isn't credited frequently. The fact that custom claims you have one year to live and that your neighbor has twenty years to live does not mean you are less alive than is your neighbor; does not mean that your enjoyment of the sunshine remaining to you need be poorer in quality than the enjoyment of your neighbor, does not mean that you need rejoice less than your neighbor rejoices at the friskiness of happy animals, at the warmth, wit and wonder of children.

Often now, I'm the oldest one in a room. It feels a little odd — if I'm made aware of it. The <u>fact</u> of it is impressive, too! I believe that people my age and people older should continue to involve themselves in the challenges, pains, comforts and responsibilities of this world.

I say to Old People: What those <u>other</u> people are doing out there affects you. Act. You can act from a wheel-chair or a sick-bed. You can act as long as you are alert and moving at all. To act does not mean to GALLOP. (necessarily!) A grin, a hand-clasp or, if you can manage it, a piece of wisdom from the breadth of your impressive experience can operate as <u>important</u> <u>act</u>.

You are alive until you are dead. Ten minutes before you're dead you're alive. You COULD save the world in ten minutes. It's a Possiblity. You are alive until the END of the split second of your death. BRAVO!

Written by Gwendolyn Brooks in the last years of her life, this previously unpublished work is recorded exactly as she penned it.

The Blackstone Rangers

I

As Seen By Disciplines

There they are.
Thirty at the corner.
Black, raw, ready.
Sores in the city
that do not want to heal.

Song: White Powder

They want me to take the white powder.
I won't, so they beat me.

They want me to deal the white powder.
I won't, so they beat me.

They tell me I'll hot-pile the Money.
They tell me my Power will roll.
They tell me I'll rule my own runners.
I'll be Mighty. I'll be
IN CONTROL.

When I say "Hot at eleven, cold before twelve"
They beat me.

AL

I Am A Black

According to my Teachers,
I am now an African-American.

They call me out of my name.

BLACK is an open umbrella.
I am Black and A Black forever.

I am one of The Blacks.

We are Here, we are There.
We occur in Brazil, in Nigeria, Ghana,
in Botswana, Tanzania, in Kenya,
in Russia, Australia, in Haiti, Soweto,
in Grenada, in Cuba, in Panama, Libya,
in England and Italy, France.

We are graces in any places.
I am Black and A Black
forever.

I am other than Hyphenation.

I say, proudly, MY PEOPLE!
I say, proudly, OUR PEOPLE!

Our People do not disdain to eat yams or melons or grits
or to put peanut butter in stew.

I am Kojo. In West Afrika Kojo
means Unconquerable. My parents
named me the seventh day from my birth
in Black spirit, Black faith, Black communion.
I am Kojo. I am A Black.
And I Capitalize my name.

Do not call me out of my name.

Big Bessie throws her son into the street

A day of sunny face and temper.
The winter trees
Are musical.

Bright lameness from my beautiful disease,
You have your destiny to chip and eat.

Be precise.
With something better than candles in the eyes.
(Candles are not enough.)

At the root of the will, a wild inflammable stuff.

New pioneer of days and ways, be gone.
Hunt out your own or make your own alone.

Go down the street.

The Boy Died in My Alley

to Running Boy

The Boy died in my alley
without my Having Known.
Policeman said, next morning,
"Apparently died Alone."

"You heard a shot?," Policeman said.
Shots I hear and Shots I hear.
I never see the Dead.

The Shot that killed him yes I heard
as I heard the Thousand shots before;
careening tinnily down the nights
across my years and arteries.

Policeman pounded on my door.
"Who is it?" "POLICE!" Policeman yelled.
"A Boy was dying in your alley.
A Boy is dead, and in your alley.
And have you known this Boy before?"

I have known this Boy before.
I have known this Boy before, who
ornaments my alley.
I never saw his face at all.
I never saw his futurefall.
But I have known this Boy.

I have always heard him deal with death.
I have always heard the shout, the volley.
I have closed my heart-ears late and early.
And I have killed him ever.

I joined the Wild and killed him
with knowledgeable unknowing.
I saw where he was going.
I saw him Crossed. And seeing,
I did not take him down.

He cried not only "Father!"
but "Mother!
Sister!
Brother."
The cry climbed up the alley.
It went up to the wind.
It hung upon the heaven
for a long
stretch-strain of Moment.

The red floor of my alley
is a special speech to me.

The Near–Johannesburg Boy

*In South Africa the Black
children ask each other:
"Have you been detained yet?
How many times have you been
detained?"*

_____

*The herein boy does not live
in Johannesburg. He is not
allowed to live there. Perhaps
he lives in Soweto.*

My way is from woe to wonder.
A Black boy near Johannesburg, hot
in the Hot Time.

Those people
do not like Black among the colors.
They do not like our
calling our country ours.
They say our country is not ours.

Those people.
Visiting the world as I visit the world.
Those people.
Their bleach is puckered and cruel.

It is work to speak to my Father. My Father.
His body was whole till they Stopped it.
Suddenly.
With a short shot.
But, before that, physically tall and among us,
he died every day. Every moment.
My father....
First was the crumpling.
No. First was the Fist-and-the-Fury.
Last was the crumpling. It is
a little used rag that is Under, it is not,
it is not my Father gone down.

About my Mother. My Mother
was this loud laugher
below sunshine, below the starlight at festival.
My Mother is still this loud laugher!
Still moving straight in the Getting-It-Done (as she names it.)
Oh a strong eye is my Mother.
Except when it seems we are lax in our looking.

Well, enough of slump, enough of Old Story.
Like a clean spear of Fire
I am moving. I am not still. I am ready
to be ready.
I shall flail
in the Hot Time.

Tonight I walk with
a hundred of playmates to where
the hurt Black of our skin is forbidden.
There, in the dark that is our dark, there,
a-pulse across earth that is our earth, there,
there exulting, there Exactly, there redeeming, there
    Roaring Up
(oh my Father)
we shall forge with the Fist-and-the-Fury:
we shall flail in the Hot Time:
we shall
we shall

The Sermon On The Warpland

"The fact that we are black
is our ultimate reality."

—Ron Karenga

And several strengths from drowsiness campaigned
but spoke in Single Sermon on the Warpland.

And went about the warpland saying No.
"My people, black and black, revile the River.
Say that the River turns, and turn the River.

Say that our Something in doublepod contains
seeds for the coming hell and health together.
Prepare to meet
(sisters, brothers) the brash and terrible weather;
the pains;
the bruising; the collapse of bestials, idols.
But then oh then!—the stuffing of the hulls!
the seasoning of the perilously sweet!
the health! the heralding of the clear obscure!

Build now your Church, my brothers, sisters. Build
never with brick nor Corten nor with granite.
Build with lithe love. With love like lion-eyes.
With love like morningrise.
With love like black, our black—
luminously indiscreet;
complete; continuous."

Paul Robeson

That time
we all heard it,
cool and clear,
cutting across the hot grit of the day.
The major Voice.
The adult Voice
forgoing Rolling River,
forgoing tearful tale of bale and barge
and other symptoms of an old despond.
Warning, in music-words
devout and large,
that we are each other's
harvest:
we are each other's
business:
we are each other's
magnitude and bond.

BLACK LOVE

Black love, provide the adequate electric
for what is lapsed and lenient in us now.

Rouse us from blur, Call us.

Call adequately the postponed corner brother.
And call our man in the pin-stripe suiting and restore
him to his abler logic; to his people.

Call to the shattered sister and repair her
in her difficult hour, narrow her fever.

Call to the Elders—
our customary grace and further sun
loved in the Long-ago, loathed in the Lately;
a luxury of languish and of rust.

Appraise, assess our Workers in the Wild, lest they
descend to malformation and to undertow.
Black love, define and escort our young, be means and
redemption, discipline.

Nourish our children—proud, strong
little men upright-easy:
quick
flexed
little stern-warm historywomen. . . .
I see them in Ghana, Kenya, in the city of Dar-es-
       Salaam, in Kalamazoo, Mound Bayou, in Chicago.

Lovely loving children
with long soft eyes.

Black love, prepare us all for interruptions;
assaults, unwanted pauses; furnish for leavings and
      for losses.

Just come out Blackly glowing!

On the ledges—in the lattices—against the failing
      light of
candles that stutter,
and in the chop and challenge of our apprehension—
be
the Alwayswonderful of this world.

To Those of My Sisters Who Kept Their Naturals

Never to look
a hot comb in the teeth.

Sisters!
I love you.
Because you love you.
Because you are erect.
Because you are also bent.
In season, stern, kind.
Crisp, soft—in season.
And you withhold.
And you extend.
And you Step out.
And you go back.
And you extend again.
Your eyes, loud-soft, with crying and
    with smiles,
are older than a million years.
And they are young.
You reach, in season.
You subside, in season.
And All
below the richrough righttime of your hair.

54

You have not bought Blondine.
You have not hailed the hot-comb recently.
You never worshipped Marilyn Monroe.
You say: Farrah's hair is hers.
You have not wanted to be white.
Nor have you testified to adoration of that
     state
with the advertisement of imitation
(*never* successful because the hot-comb is
     laughing too.)

But oh the rough dark Other music!
the Real,
the Right.
The natural Respect of Self and Seal!
     Sisters!
Your hair is Celebration in the world!

AURORA

"the early period of anything"
Webster

We who are weak and wonderful, wicked, bewildered, wistful and wild
are saying direct Good mornings through the fever.

It is the giant-hour.
Nothing less than gianthood will do:
nothing less than mover, prover, shover, cover, lever, diver,
for giant tacklings, overturnings, new
organic staring
that will involve, that will involve us all.

We say direct Good-mornings through the fever.
across the brooding obliques, the somersaults, ashes,
across
the importances stylishly killed:
across
the edited bias.
the waffling of woman.
the structured rejection of blackness.

Ready for ways.
windows:
remodeling spirals; closing the hot cliches.
Unwinding witchcraft.

Opening to sun.

Cool Weather

We Real Cool

THE POOL PLAYERS.
SEVEN AT THE GOLDEN SHOVEL.

We real cool. We
Left school. We

Lurk late. We
Strike straight. We

Sing sin. We
Thin gin. We

Jazz June. We
Die soon.

About We Real Cool
(Notes from Nora)

My mother often provided background to this well-known poem, telling audiences about passing a pool hall *(on 75th street in Chicago, east of Cottage Grove Avenue)* not far from our home. *(The pool hall was not named "The Golden Shovel" and she arbitrarily picked the number seven.)* The young-ish boys playing pool should have been in school.

In her 1st autobiography, <u>*Report From Part One,*</u> she said "the boys have no accented sense of themselves, yet they are aware of a semi-defined personal importance" which is why the word "we" should be said softly. The break after each "we" was there to represent the gasp of an impending existential or actual death.

And while this is by no means a bright and bubbly poem, there was a moment in her explanation that often amused the crowd. She created the phrase "jazz June" because the improvisations of jazz run counter to the mildness of June. However, the poem was banned in several places because people assumed her use of the word *jazz* had some sort of sexual reference. She frequently closed her pre-poem explanation with "that was not my intention though I have no objection if it helps anybody!" And laughter would ring out.

Fall

Core members of the writers' group which met at 7428 S. Evans, the home of Gwendolyn Brooks. From the left: Carolyn Rodgers, Sharon Scott, Johari Amini, Mike Cook, Gwendolyn Brooks, Walter Bradford, Don L. Lee *(now Haki Madhubuti)*

old laughter

The men and women long ago
In Africa, in Africa,
Knew all there was of joy to know.
In sunny Africa
The spices flew from tree to tree.
The spices trifled in the air.
That carelessly
Fondled the twisted hair.

The men and women richly sang
In land of gold and green and red.
The bells of merriment richly rang.

But richness is long dead,
Old laughter chilled, old music done
In bright, bewildered Africa.

The bamboo and the cinnamon
Are sad in Africa.

Parents
from <u>Report From Part Two</u>

Home always warmly awaited us. Welcoming, endorsing. Home meant a quick-walking, careful, duty-loving, never-surly mother, who had been a schoolteacher, who played the piano, sang in a high soprano, and wrote music to which I wrote the words, made fudge, made cocoa and prune whip and apricot pie, drew tidy cows and trees and expert houses with chimneys and chimney smoke, who helped her children with arithmetic homework. Home meant my father, a janitor for McKinley Music Company. He had kind eyes, songs, and tense recitations for my brother and myself. We never tired of his stories and story poems. My father seemed to Gwendolyn and Raymond a figure of Power. He had those rich Artistic Abilities, but he had more. He could fix anything that broke or stopped. He could build long-lasting fires in the ancient furnace below. He could paint the house, inside and out, and could whitewash the basement. He could spread the American Flag in wide loud clean magic across the front of our house on the Fourth of July and on Declaration Day. He could chuckle. No one has ever had, no one will ever have, a chuckle exactly like my father's. It was gentle, it was warmly happy it was heavyish but not hard. It was secure and seemed to us an assistant to the Power that registered with his children, always, as magic. My father, too, was almost our family doctor.

We had Dr. Carter, of course, precise and semi-twinkly and efficient—but it was not always necessary to call him. My father had wanted to be a doctor. Thwarted after one year's training, he read every "doctor book" he could reach, learning fine secrets and curing us with steams, and fruit compotes, and dexterous rubs, and, above all, with bedside compassion. "Well, there, young lady! How's that throat now? Well, let's see. This salve will take care of that bruise! Now we're going to be all right." In illness there was an advantage: the invalid was royalty for the run of the seizure.

MAMA!—telling me when I showed her, at seven, a page of rhymes: "You're going to be the lady Paul Laurence Dunbar!" Star-bits in her eyes! She and my father praised me to anyone who visited the house. And my mother praised me to Langston Hughes. She made me show my poems to him when he came to recite at our church, Metropolitan Community Church in Chicago. And she praised me to James Weldon Johnson, author of "God's Trombones," when he came to a *fancier* church: her assault was—"SHE'S the one who sent you all those wonderful poems." The great Dr. Johnson drew himself up, which he had every right to do, crossed his hands in front of him. "I get so many OF them, you kno-OW, "was his textured response. Our encounter with Langston, though, was comfortable, regenerative. "You're very talented!" he exclaimed. "Keep writing! Some day you'll have a book published!"

The Bean Eaters

They eat beans mostly, this old yellow pair.
Dinner is a casual affair.
Plain chipware on a plain and creaking wood,
Tin flatware.

Two who are Mostly Good.
Two who have lived their day,
But keep on putting on their clothes
And putting things away.

And remembering . . .
Remembering, with twinklings and twinges,
As they lean over the beans in their rented back room that
      is full of beads and receipts and dolls and cloths,
      tobacco crumbs, vases and fringes.

old people working (garden, car)

Old people working. Making a gift of garden.
Or washing a car, so some one else may ride.
A note of alliance, an eloquence of pride.
A way of greeting or sally to the world.

when you have forgotten Sunday: the love story

—And when you have forgotten the bright bedclothes
    on a Wednesday and a Saturday,
And most especially when you have forgotten Sunday—
When you have forgotten Sunday halves in bed,
Or me sitting on the front-room radiator in the limping
    afternoon
Looking off down the long street
To nowhere,
Hugged by my plain old wrapper of no-expectation
And nothing-I-have-to-do and I'm-happy-why?
And if-Monday-never-had-to-come—
When you have forgotten that, I say,
And how you swore, if somebody beeped the bell,
And how my heart played hopscotch if the telephone rang;
And how we finally went in to Sunday dinner,
That is to say, went across the front room floor to the
    ink-spotted table in the southwest corner
To Sunday dinner, which was always chicken and noodles
Or chicken and rice
And salad and rye bread and tea
And chocolate chip cookies—

I say, when you have forgotten that,
When you have forgotten my little presentiment
That the war would be over before they got to you;
And how we finally undressed and whipped out the
    light and flowed into bed,
And lay loose-limbed for a moment in the week-end
Bright bedclothes,
Then gently folded into each other—
When you have, I say, forgotten all that,
Then you may tell,
Then I may believe
You have forgotten me well.

Beverly Hills, Chicago

("and the people live till they have white hair" E. M. PRICE)

The dry brown coughing beneath their feet,
(Only a while, for the handyman is on his way)
These people walk their golden gardens.
We say ourselves fortunate to be driving by today.

That we may look at them, in their gardens where
The summer ripeness rots. But not raggedly.
Even the leaves fall down in lovelier patterns here.
And the refuse, the refuse is a neat brilliancy.

When they flow sweetly into their houses
With softness and slowness touched by that everlasting gold,
We know what they go to. To tea. But that does not mean
They will throw some little black dots into some water and
    add sugar and the juice of the cheapest lemons that
    are sold,

While downstairs that woman's vague phonograph bleats,
    "Knock me a kiss."
And the living all to be made again in the sweatingest
    physical manner
Tomorrow....Not that anybody is saying that these people
    have no trouble.
Merely that it is trouble with a gold-flecked beautiful
    banner.

72

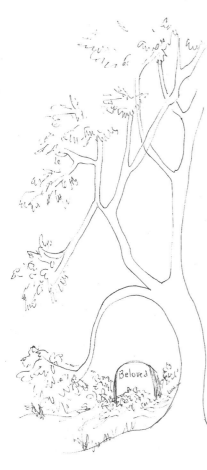

Nobody is saying that these people do not ultimately cease
    to be. And
Sometimes their passings are even more painful than ours.
It is just that so often they live till their hair is white.
They make excellent corpses, among the expensive
    flowers....

Nobody is furious. Nobody hates these people.
At least, nobody driving by in this car.
It is only natural, however, that it should occur to us
How much more fortunate they are than we are.

It is only natural that we should look and look
At their wood and brick and stone
And think, while a breath of pine blows,
How different these are from our own.

We do not want them to have less.
But it is only natural that we should think we have not
    enough.
We drive on, we drive on.
When we speak to each other our voices are a little gruff.

kitchenette building

WE ARE things of dry hours and the involuntary plan,
Grayed in, and gray. "Dream" makes a giddy sound, not
    strong
Like "rent," "feeding a wife," satisfying a man."

But could a dream send up through onion fumes
Its white and violet, fight with fried potatoes
And yesterday's garbage ripening in the hall,
Flutter, or sing an aria down these rooms

Even if we were willing to let it in,
Had time to warm it, keep it very clean,
Anticipate a message, let it begin?

We wonder. But not well! not for a minute!
Since Number Five is out of the bathroom now,
We think of lukewarm water, hope to get in it.

Maud Martha Spares the Mouse

THERE. She had it at last. The weeks it had devoted to eluding her, the tricks; the clever hide-and-go-seeks, the routes it had in all sobriety devised, together with the delicious moments it had, undoubtedly, laughed up its sleeve—all to no ultimate avail. She had that mouse.

It shook its little self, as best it could, in the trap. Its bright black eyes contained no appeal—the little creature seemed to understand that there was no hope of mercy from the eternal enemy, no hope of reprieve or postponement—but a fine small dignity. It waited. It looked at Maud Martha.

She wondered what else it was thinking. Perhaps that there was not enough food in its larder. Perhaps that little Betty, a puny child from the start, would not, now, be getting fed. Perhaps that, now, the family's seasonal house-cleaning, for lack of expert direction, would be left undone. It might be regretting that young Bobby's education was now at an end. It might be nursing personal regrets. No more the mysterious shadows of the kitchenette, the uncharted twists, and the unguessed halls. No more the sweet delights of the chase, the charms of being unsuccessfully hounded, thrown at.

Maud Martha could not bear the little look.

"Go home to your children," she urged. "To your wife or husband." She opened the trap. The mouse vanished.

Suddenly, she was conscious of a new cleanness in her. A wide air walked in her. A life had blundered its way into her power and it had been hers to preserve or destroy. She had not destroyed. In the center of that simple restraint was—creation. She had created a piece of life. It was wonderful.

"Why," she thought, as her height doubled, "why, I'm good! I am *good*."

She ironed her aprons. Her back was straight. Her eyes were mild, and soft with a godlike loving—kindness.

Clement Lewy

Then there was Clement Lewy, a little boy at the back, on the second floor.

Lewy life was not terrifically tossed. Saltless, rather. Or like an unmixed batter. Lumpy.

Little Clement's mother had grown listless after the desertion. She looked as though she had been scrubbed, up and down, on the washing board, doused from time to time in gray and noisome water. But little Clement looked alert, he looked happy, he was always spirited. He was in second grade. He did his work, and had always been promoted. At home he sang. He recited little poems. He told his mother little stories wound out of the air by himself. His mother glanced at him once in a while. She would have been proud of him if she had had the time.

She started toward her housemaid's work each morning at seven. She left a glass of milk and a bowl of dry cereal and a dish of prunes on the table, and set the alarm clock for eight. At eight little Clement punched off the alarm, stretched, got up, washed, dressed, combed, brushed, ate his breakfast. It was quiet in the apartment. He hurried off to school. At noon he returned from school, opened the door with his key. It was quiet in the apartment. He poured himself a second glass of milk, got more prunes, and ate a slice—"just one slice," his mother had cautioned—of bread and butter. He went back to school. At three o'clock he returned from school, opened the door with his key. It was quiet in the apartment. He got a couple of graham crackers out of the cookie can. He drew himself a glass of water. He changed his clothes. Then he went out to play, leaving behind him the two rooms. Leaving behind him the brass beds, the lamp with the faded silk tassel and frayed cord, the hooked oven door, the cracks in the walls and the quiet. As he played, he kept a lookout for his mother, who usually arrived at seven, or near that hour. When he saw her rounding the corner, his little face underwent a transformation. His eyes lashed into brightness, his lips opened suddenly and became a smile, and his eyebrows climbed toward his hairline in relief and joy.

He would run to his mother and almost throw his little body at her. "Here I am, mother! Here I am! Here I am!"

A Sunset of the City

Kathleen Eileen

Already I am no longer looked at with lechery or love.
My daughters and sons have put me away with marbles and dolls,
Are gone from the house.
My husband and lovers are pleasant or somewhat polite
And night is night.

It is a real chill out,
The genuine thing.
I am not deceived, I do not think it is still summer
Because sun stays and birds continue to sing.

It is summer-gone that I see, it is summer-gone.
The sweet flowers indrying and dying down,
The grasses forgetting their blaze and consenting to brown.

It is a real chill out. The fall crisp comes.
I am aware there is winter to heed.
There is no warm house
That is fitted with my need.

I am cold in this cold house this house
Whose washed echoes are tremulous down lost halls.
I am a woman, and dusty, standing among new affairs.
I am a woman who hurries through her prayers.

Tin intimations of a quiet core to be my
Desert and my dear relief
Come: there shall be such islanding from grief,
And small communion with the master shore.
Twang they. And I incline this ear to tin,
Consult a dual dilemma. Whether to dry
In humming pallor or to leap and die.

Somebody muffed it? Somebody wanted to joke.

Patrick Bouie of Cabrini Green

What is devout is never to forget.
Never to shelve the value and the beauty.

Patrick.
Vivid. Valid. Lyrical.

We cannot reach,
We cannot touch.

The radiant richness that was Patrick
Cannot be reached again, cannot be hugged.
   Cannot be visited.

What is devout is never to forget
that he was with us for a little while.
Our splendor.
Our creative spirit.
Our sparkling contribution. Our
flash of Influence interrupted.

   Our Interrupted Man.

Martin Luther King Jr.
April 4, 1968

A man went forth with gifts.
He was a prose poem.
He was a tragic grace.
He was a warm music.
He tried to heal the vivid volcanoes.
His ashes are
      reading the world.
His Dream still wishes to anoint
the barricades of faith and of control.
His word still burns the center of the sun,
      above the thousands and the
      hundred thousands.
The word was Justice. It was spoken.
So it shall be spoken.
So it shall be done.

MALCOLM X

for Dudley Randall

Original.
Ragged-round,
Rich-robust.

He had the hawk-man's eyes.
We gasped. We saw the maleness.
The maleness raking out and making guttural the air
and pushing us to walls.

And in a soft and fundamental hour
A sorcery devout and vertical
beguiled the world.

He opened us—
who was a key,

who was a man.

Behind the Scenes

When I see a President, a Vice President, a Secretary of
State on sparkling tile,
beside noble columns of white,
I think to myself: "Somebody got there early,
and swept, and scrubbed; somebody dusted."

Before the President came,
somebody buffed his shoes.
The not too-stiffened white of his shirt
was not achieved by his own agility.

At the invisible controls: some little
weak-kneed, stricken, or powerful woman or man.

An Aspect of Love, Alive in the Ice and Fire

LaBohem Brown

In a package of minutes there is this We.
How beautiful.
Merry foreigners in our morning,
we laugh, we touch each other,
are responsible props and posts.

A physical light is in the room.

Because the world is at the window
we cannot wonder very long.

You rise. Although
genial, you are in yourself again.
I observe
your direct and respectable stride.
You are direct and self-accepting as a lion
in Afrikan velvet. You are level, lean,
remote.

There is a moment in Camaraderie
when interruption is not to be understood.
I cannot bear an interruption.
This is the shining joy;
the time of not-to-end.

On the street we smile.
We go
in different directions
down the imperturbable street.

Infirm

Everybody here
is infirm.
Everybody here is infirm.
Oh. Mend me. Mend me. Lord.

Today I
say to them
say to them
say to them, Lord:
look! I am beautiful, beautiful with
my wing that is wounded
my eye that is bonded
or my ear not funded
or my walk all a-wobble.
I'm enough to be beautiful.

You are
beautiful too.

Winter

Gwendolyn Brooks and famed historian, Lerone Bennett, Jr.

Cynthia In The Snow

It SUSHES.
It hushes
The loudness in the road.
It flitter-twitters,
And laughs away from me.
It laughs a lovely whiteness,
And whitely whirs away,
To be
Some otherwhere,
Still white as milk or shirts.
So beautiful it hurts.

Pete at the Zoo

I wonder if the elephant
Is lonely in his stall
When all the boys and girls are gone
And there's no shout at all,
And there's no one to stamp before,
No one to note his might.
Does he hunch up, as I do,
Against the dark of night?

the children of the poor
2

What shall I give my children? who are poor,
Who are adjudged the leastwise of the land,
Who are my sweetest lepers, who demand
No velvet and no velvety velour;
But who have begged me for a brisk contour,
Crying that they are quasi, contraband
Because unfinished, graven by a hand
Less than angelic, admirable or sure.
My hand is stuffed with mode, design, device.
But I lack access to my proper stone.
And plenitude of plan shall not suffice
Nor grief nor love shall be enough alone
To ratify my little halves who bear
Across an autumn freezing everywhere.

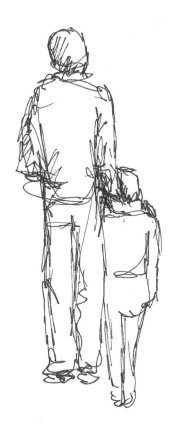

Uncle Seagram

My uncle likes me too much.

I am five and a half years old, and in kindergarten.
In kindergarten everything is clean.

My uncle is six feet tall with seven bumps on his chin.
My uncle is six feet tall, and he stumbles.
He stumbles because of his Wonderful Medicine
packed in his pocket all times.

Family is ma and pa and my uncle,
three brothers, three sisters, and me.

Every night at my house we play checkers and dominoes.
My uncle sits <u>close</u>.
There aren't any shoes or socks on his feet.
Under the table a big toe tickles my ankle.
Under the oilcloth his thin knee beats into mine.
And mashes. And mashes.

When we look at TV
my uncle picks <u>me</u> to sit on his lap.
As I sit, he gets hard in the middle.
I squirm, but he keeps me, and kisses my ear.

I am not even a girl.

Once, when I went to the bathroom,
my uncle noticed, came in, shut the door,
put his long white tongue in my ear,
and whispered "We're Best Friends, and Family.
and we know how to keep Secrets."

My uncle likes me too much. I am worried.

I do not like my uncle anymore.

Thinking of Elizabeth Steinberg

Friday, November 13, 1987.

Already you're on Page 8.
And in a while your name will not be remembered
by that large animal The Public General.

I don't know who will remember you, Lisa,
or consider the big fists breaking your little bones,
or consider the vague bureaucrats
stumbling, fumbling through Paper.

Your given name is my middle name, Elizabeth.
But that is not why I am sick when I think of you
     There—
no one to help you in
your private horror of monsters and Fools.

You are the world's Little Girl.
And what is a Little Girl for?
She is for putting a bow-ribbon on.
She is for paper dolls.
She is for playmates and birthday parties.
She is to love, to love.

She is to be precious, precious.
She is for ice cream cones.

She is not to be hurt.
She is not to be pounded.

Elizabeth, Lisa.
We cannot help you.

They wept at the wake in Redden's Funeral Home,
among messages, bright gladiolas.
There was weeping at your grave.

Tardy tears
will not return you to air.

But if you are Somewhere, and sentient,
be comforted, little spirit.
Because of your lean day,
the vulgarity of your storm,
the erosion and rot of your masters, sitting in the
    sputum of their souls—
another Lisa
will not die.

You help us begin to hear.
We begin to hear the scream out of the twisted mouth,
and
out of the eye, that strives to be Normal.

We shall listen, listen.
We shall stomp into the Horror Houses,
invade the caves of the monsters.

In the name of Elizabeth Steinberg.
In the name of
Lisa.

To Be Grown Up

The whole chocolate cake can be yours.

To be grown up means
you don't get a report card.
You don't face a father, a mother.

The walls of the cage are gone.
The fortress is done and down.

To be grown up means
the Bill will be paid by you.

To be grown up means
you can get sick and stay sick.
Your legs will not love you. They'll fail.

No icy sidewalks for sliding.

No grandmother to fix you big biscuits.
No grandfather to sing you "Asleep in the Deep."

The Crazy Woman

I shall not sing a May song.
A May song should be gay.
I'll wait until November
And sing a song of gray.

I'll wait until November.
That is the time for me.
I'll go out in the frosty dark
And sing most terribly.

And all the little people
Will stare at me and say,
"That is the Crazy Woman
Who would not sing in May."

An Old Black Woman, Homeless, And Indistinct

1.

Your every day is a pilgrimage.
A blue hubbub.
Your days are collected bacchanals of fear and self-troubling.

And your nights! Your nights.
When you put you down in alley or cardboard or viaduct,
your lovers are rats, finding your secret places.

2.

When you rise in another morning,
you hit the street, your incessant enemy.

See? Here you are, in the so-busy world.
You walk. You walk.
You pass The People.
No. The People pass you.

Here's a Rich Girl marching briskly to her charms.
She is suede and scarf and belting and perfume.
She sees you not, she sees you very well.
At five in the afternoon Miss Rich girl will go Home
to brooms and vacuum cleaner and carpeting,
two cats, two marble-top tables, two telephones,
shiny green peppers, flowers in impudent vases,
visitors.
Before all that there's luncheon to be known.
Lasagna, lobster salad, sandwiches.
All day there's coffee to be loved.
There are luxuries
of minor dissatisfaction, luxuries of Plan.

3.

That's <u>her</u> story,
<u>You're</u> going to vanish, not necessarily nicely, fairly soon,
Although essentially dignity itself a death
is not necessarily tidy, modest or discreet.
When they find you
your legs may not be tidy nor aligned.
Your mouth may be all crooked or destroyed.

Black old woman, homeless, indistinct_
Your last and least adventure is Review.
      Folks used to celebrate your birthday!
Folks used to say "She's such a pretty little thing!"
Folks used to say "She draws such handsome horses, cows and houses,"
Folks used to say "That child is going far."

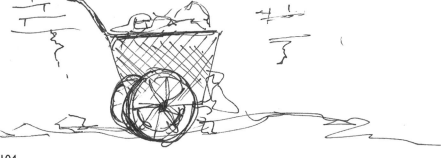

September, 1992.

my dreams, my works, must wait till after hell

I hold my honey and I store my bread
In little jars and cabinets of my will.
I label clearly, and each latch and lid
I bid, Be firm till I return from hell.
I am very hungry. I am incomplete.
And none can tell when I may dine again.
No man can give me any word but Wait,
The puny light. I keep eyes pointed in;
Hoping that, when the devil days of my hurt
Drag out to their last dregs and I resume
On such legs as are left me, in such heart
As I can manage, remember to go home,
My taste will not have turned insensitive
To honey and bread old purity could love.

To Black Women

Sisters,
where there is cold silence —
no hallelujahs, no hurrahs at all, no handshakes,
no neon red or blue, no smiling faces —
prevail.
Prevail across the editors of the world!
who are obsessed, self-honeying and self-crowned
in the seduced arena.

　　　　It has been a
hard trudge, with fainting, bandaging and death.
There have been startling confrontations.
There have been tramplings. Tramplings
of monarchs and of other men.

But there remain large countries in your eyes.
Shrewd sun.
The civil balance.
The listening secrets.

And you create and train your flowers still.

of De Witt Williams on his way to Lincoln Cemetery

He was born in Alabama.
He was bred in Illinois.
He was nothing but a
Plain black boy.

Swing low swing low sweet sweet chariot.
Nothing but a plain black boy.

Drive him past the Pool Hall.
Drive him past the Show.
Blind within his casket,
But maybe he will know.

Down through Forty-seventh Street:
Underneath the L,
And—Northwest Corner, Prairie,
That he loved so well.

Don't forget the Dance Halls—
Warwick and Savoy,
Where he picked his women, where
He drank his liquid joy.

Born In Alabama.
Bred in Illinois.
He was nothing but a
Plain black boy.

Swing low swing low sweet sweet chariot.
Nothing but a plain black boy.

IX
Truth

And if sun comes
How shall we greet him?
Shall we not dread him,
Shall we not fear him
After so lengthy a
Session with shade?

Though we have wept for him,
Though we have prayed
All through the night-years—
What if we wake one shimmering morning to
Hear the fierce hammering
Of his firm knuckles Hard on the door?

Shall we not shudder?—
Shall we not flee
Into the shelter, the dear thick shelter
Of the familiar
Propitious haze?

Sweet is it, sweet is it
To sleep in the coolness
Of snug unawareness.

The dark hangs heavily
Over the eyes.

Aloneness

Aloneness is different from loneliness.
Loneliness means you want somebody

Loneliness means
you have not planned to stand
somewhere with other people gone.

Loneliness never has a bright color.
                    Perhaps it is gray.

Loneliness does not
            have a lovely sound.

It has an under buzz.
            Or it does not have a sound.

When it does not have a sound
        I like it least of all.

But aloneness is delicious.
Sometimes aloneness is delicious.

Once in a while aloneness is delicious.
                Almost like a red small apple
         that is cold. An apple that is small
                and sweet and round and cold
                          and for just you.

Or like loving a pond in summer.

There is the soft water,
looking a little silver-dark, and kind.

You lean, most carefully,
and you like the single picture there.

Rest is under your eyes
and above your eyes
and your brain stops its wrinkles
and is peaceful as a windless pond.

You make presents to yourself,
presents of clouds and sunshine,
and the dandelions that are there.

Aloneness is like that. Sometimes.

Sometimes
    I think it is not possible
                 to be alone.

You are with you.

And pulse and nature
keep you company.

The little minutes are there,
building into hours:

the minutes that are the bricks
of days and years.

I know another aloneness.

Within it there is someone.
Someone to ask and tell.

One who is Mary, Willie,
John or James or Joan.

Whose other name is Love.

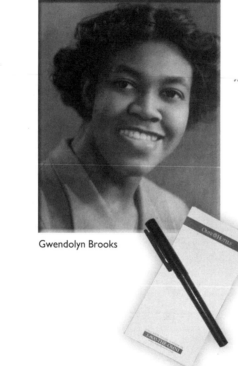

Gwendolyn Brooks

"I am a writer perhaps because I am not a talker. It has always been hard for me to say exactly what I mean in speech But if I have written a clumsiness, I may erase it."

-Gwendolyn Brooks

Memories

As she went along her way...
(a sampling of contents from the travel bags of Gwendolyn Brooks)

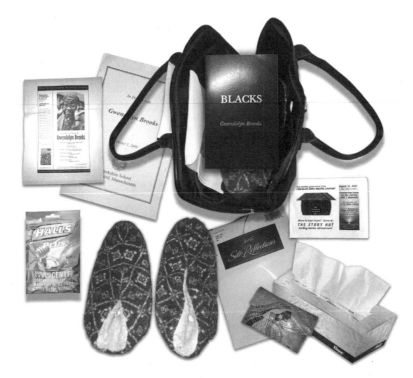

_____A memory from...

Nora Brooks Blakely

So many, many memories but here's one that amazed me when mama shared it.

My mother loved going to elementary schools and high schools. There are countless stories about her encouragement of young writers and enthusiasm for young readers. Numerous occasions where she was inspired by the literary voices of children and created poetry contests with monetary awards on the spot.

One day she went to a small elementary school in Chicago and read to the entire student body. Everyone was excited about meeting GWENDOLYN BROOKS and they all wanted autographs. So she sat down and signed autographs for each and everyone of the 400+ children that attended the school. Every. One.

What amazes me *(to this day!)* is the fact that she mentioned this to me in passing. It was not the "lead" in her story about her experiences at the school. She wasn't looking for applause. It was simply something that was important to the children and so it was important to her. Many people give lip service to a commitment to young people and "giving back" but this was one of the many ways mama demonstrated her deep and abiding commitment to Youth and to Art.

Cynthia A. Walls

I have many memories of Mrs. Blakely but the one that stands out to me is the first time I had dinner at the Blakely home. I met Mr. and Mrs. Blakely after a show I had performed in at Kuumba Theatre. Shortly thereafter Nora, their daughter and my best friend, told me that I had been invited to dinner. I said yes but I shivered from the time of the invitation to the time of the dinner. I sat there in disbelief thinking "I can't believe I am really sitting in the home of Gwendolyn Brooks." The atmosphere was very warm and inviting and she was so real and down to earth. As the evening progressed I relaxed a little more. But then came the moment when all my anxiety was freed. Gwen told her favorite joke.

Ten Toreadors, one bull
 Nine Toreadors, one bull
    Eight Toreadors, one bull
      Seven Toreadors, one bull
        Six Toreadors, one bull
          Five Toreadors, one bull
            Four Toreadors, one bull
              Three Toreadors, one bull
                Two Toreadors, one bull
                  One Toreador, one bull

One bull

At the end of the joke she let out a very hearty chuckle. That joke and chuckle eased my fear and introduced me to my friend Gwen. Yes, there are so many memories I have of Gwen but that was one of my first. By the way I love telling that joke.

Haki R. Madhubuti

When I was still Don L. Lee, Gwendolyn Brooks came into my life. She pretty much adopted me as a project and family member. After I got the position at Cornell University as Black poet-in-residence Gwen and I would occasionally travel together to readings. These places had invited her and she had them put me on the program. I remember particularly the one at the University of Pittsburgh where the place was just packed. Moneta Sleet, the Ebony photographer was there, and I think David Llorens, who had decided to do this article on me for *Ebony* magazine, was there. She read, she introduced me and I read. I'm thinking to myself there's something wrong with this picture.

What was essentially wrong with this picture then and, as I continued to grow and to get over myself, was realizing the importance of Gwendolyn Brooks allowing me to come into her family. I wasn't gonna let this happen anymore. I will read first and then introduce her. That's the African way. She is the elder in the community.

She was always very kind to me. In fact, one of the only couple of times I remember Gwen being angry with me was when I changed my name to Haki Madhubuti. She did not go along with that at first. She felt we had worked so hard for Don L. Lee we should have kept that as my name, kind of a brand. But from that point on we were always on the same page.

Paulette Brooks

Gwendolyn Brooks was my aunt, my father's only sister and my grandparents' only daughter. I had no idea my aunt was *"Gwendolyn Brooks,"* the most accomplished Black poet of the time. I went to Catholic school and I don't recall having any type of Black History observances in those days, and unfortunately, I don't remember my school ever educating us about Black achievements.

What I remember most about my Aunt and the rest of my family is being at my grandparents' home every holiday and loving it. Christmas, Thanksgiving, Easter, every important yearly holiday celebration. Nora and I learning how to set the table *(a tradition that doesn't happen much anymore)* and watching my grandmother prepare dishes that I still prepare today for my family. My grandmother and my aunt played the piano and we sang all of our favorite and traditional songs. Our family was small. My younger brother and sister, David and Doretha came along later so it was just Uncle Henry, Aunt Gwendolyn, Henry, Jr., Nora, Pete, Me, Mama *(Thelma)*, Daddy *(Raymond)* and of course, David and Keziah, my Grandfather and Grandmother. How I enjoyed those days of celebration, especially when the family encouraged me to sing and perform for them. They loved ballads and so did I. At the tender age of nine I memorized many popular standards of the time and would sing for their amusement at all of our holiday and traditional gatherings.

My Aunt Gwendolyn was part of it all and that's what I remember.

Quraysh Ali Lansana

Miss Brooks knew my wife Emily years before we met. A graduate of the Yale Theater School, and classmate of Angela Bassett and Charles Dutton, Emily moved to Chicago in 1988 to pursue stage and screen. Ironically, this was the same year I moved from Oklahoma to the Windy City, guided greatly by the poetry of Miss Brooks.

Emily, in 1989, auditioned for a part in a Columbia College-based theater group to perform a selection of Miss Brooks' poetry on stage. Emily landed a role in the show, and two months later found herself in a small theater on the downtown Chicago campus performing in front of the author.

After the show, Miss Brooks expressed how pleased she was with Emily's interpretation and performance. So when, in July 1993, I pulled up in front of Miss Brooks' South Shore Drive condo with Emily in the passenger seat of my Mustang, my stock instantly rose. We were at her home to deliver her to the first open mic award contest in her name, sponsored by the Guild Literary Complex, one of Chicago's oldest literary centers.

Though Miss Brooks and I had met on at least two occasions to coordinate the contest, she was most thrilled when she saw Emily step out of my small navy blue car to greet her. Flashing her contagious, and often elusive smile, she gave Emily a big hug. Then, as I guided Miss Brooks gently into the back seat, she nodded, and said simply, "I approve."

Harry Mark Petrakis

When I recall the lengthy span of our friendship with Gwendolyn Brooks and Henry Blakely, what comes foremost to mind are not poetry readings and other literary gatherings but the festive social occasions, the birthdays and holidays we celebrated together. Often we were joined by other good friends Gloria and Lerone Bennett. My wife Diana and I looked eagerly forward to these gatherings.

Both Gwendolyn and Henry had full throated and unrestrained laughs, each at a different tone level. They would freely interrupt one another. After Henry would make some extravagant assertion, Gwen would shake her head and with a slight smile say, "Oh Henry… that isn't true."

Henry would defend himself vigorously and a brisk little interplay would go back and forth between them.

Both Gwen and Henry were vigorously expressive, and when their voices were matched with the voices and laughter of Gloria and Lerone and the boisterous chatter of Diana and myself, the noise level around us was dramatically elevated. I often thought that if it were not for Gwen's celebrity we might have been thrown out of some of the restaurants where we were dining.

If I could be returned to the faith of childhood and believe as I believed then, I'd like to think that someday our group will be reunited, dining together in some heavenly settlement. If we became boisterous as we were prone to do, I can imagine one of the angels coming to warn us that if we didn't quiet down they would have to throw us all out.

Jan Spivey Gilchrist

In answer to the question given her regarding a time to phone her back, the Queen answered politely, "tell whomever to remember to phone long before or long after, my shows."

Later she named one such show, a Soap Opera I had shamefully enjoyed since high school. The words I had heard most of my life exploded in my head. *Smart people should not engage in such things.*

 I rose from my chair strong and proud, no longer ashamed. No longer afraid to be myself and own whatever made me…me.

The Queen had given me permission, as she had to everyone since 1955, at least. The same permission she had so gracefully bestowed upon the many children she had visited, written to, written about and children she had loved throughout the country and the world.

Without even realizing my presence, Gwendolyn Brooks had given me the greatest gift. A gift to take into the latter part of my life. The gift of *real* freedom.

_____A memory from...

Sandra Cisneros

A Thousand Thanks to My Teacher, Miss Brooks

I once ran into Gwendolyn Brooks in the basement of the Stop & Shop in downtown Chicago. This was when she knew me as a high school teacher and not as a writer. She was standing in line at the bakery counter looking like a mother coming home from work.

"Miss Brooks, what are you doing here?"

"I'm buying a cake," Miss Brooks said matter-of-factly.

Of course she was buying a cake. Still it didn't seem possible then that poets of her stature went downtown on the subway and bought themselves cakes. Gwendolyn Brooks was famous, maybe the most famous person I knew then, and I admired her greatly. I'd been reading her work since high school. To meet her at a university or bookstore was one thing. But here she was waiting to buy a cake! She didn't look like a Pulitzer Prize-winning author. She looked like a sparrow or nun in the modest brown and navy she always wore.

Like Elena Poniatowska, she taught me what it is to be generous to others, to speak to every member of your public as if *they* were the guest writer, and not the other way around.

This generosity and way of honoring her readers has made me see her not only as a great poet but as a great human being, and this, in my book, is the greatest kind of writer of all.

Credit: From A HOUSE OF MY OWN: STORIES FROM MY LIFE. Copyright © 2015 by Sandra Cisneros. Published by Alfred A. Knopf, a division of Penguin Random House, LLC, New York. By permission of Susan Bergholz Literary Services, New York City and Lamy, NM. All rights reserved.

_____A memory from...

Val Gray Ward

MEMORY 1

Gwen loved good restaurants.
Occasionally . . . Marshall Field's here we come!
After enjoying our lunch and girl talk she would always buy Frango Mints and chocolate chip cookies to go.

MEMORY 2

"Val! Val? Val… Val!"
"Val! You know better than to call me when I'm watching "All My Children."
Abruptly, 'bang!'
Well, then I knew not to call during "Soap Opera" time!

MEMORY 3

"Val, come over. I have an album of this wonderful new artist." It was Al Green's "Love & Happiness."
"Sunday, Al Green will be at the Amphitheatre." We went.
"Young people will fill the theatre."
Surprise! The big and little church ladies with their church hats packed the place.
We had a gooood time!

It was "Love & Happiness."

MEMORY 4

"Val, you must write your memoirs," Gwen would say to me.
"Gwendolyn, instead I'm going to quilt my memoir."
"What do you know about quilting?" she asked.
"Nothing…" I replied.
40 years later I am finishing the quilt!
Now I have to write a historical book (i.e. *"memoir"*) explaining it.

It is dedicated to you, Gwen.
You win!

125

Lerone Bennett

Gwen was fun. She loved life with a superhuman passion. She loved scents, sounds, sights, music. In an age of instant coffee, instant celebrities and instant prophets, she was a long-distance runner.

She loved her family, especially her husband. I have said many times that there are millions of married couples, but great couples, great teams that sparkle together and make everything around them sparkle are rare. Gwen and Henry were a great couple. They blended their two gifts into one and together they made one music, but more vast. Gloria and I enjoyed many warm dinners with them full of joy and laughter late into the night. At one of her husband's last dinners, Henry said with cheerful chuckles, "Gwendolyn says she is going to give a big dinner party in honor of my 80th birthday, whether I'm there or not!" She did indeed host that party posthumously, and it was a wonderful tribute!

She was a national and international treasure; a poet who became a poem.

WORDS
FOR ALL SEASONS

Young Poet's Primer

No writing primer or manual can be, in itself, complete. This little primer does not pretend to supply All You Need. You will need other books, with technical tables, analyses, philosophy. In visits to hundreds of schools and colleges, however, I have found that the enclosed ideas and impressions have proven useful. The address is chiefly to high schoolers and to college students, but elementary school teachers will find certain suggestions helpful in their classrooms — or in special efforts with talented children.

GWENDOLYN BROOKS
CHICAGO • AUGUST 30, 1980

1980!?! YES. We have included this valuable guide as inspiration and information for writers of any stripe. Now, nearly 40 years later, these tips and supports from Gwendolyn Brooks still inspire creativity and confirmation that as a writer <u>you are not alone</u>! And while a few references may be dated this is an <u>amazing</u> example of a major writer's continued relevance in the 21st-century…and beyond.

NORA BROOKS BLAKELY
CHICAGO • 2016

Young Poet's Primer
<small>(THE BOOK)</small>

1 Use fresh language.

2 But the basic of your fresh language is ordinary speech. Do not write anything that sounds like "Thou saintly skies of empyrean blue, through which there soarest sweetest bird of love." Because people do not talk that way today. (Did they ever?) Also, do not use such old-fashioned words as ecstasy, or ethereal. Do not say 'neath, ne'er. e'er, or mid. Instead, say beneath or below, say never, say ever, say *among*.

3 *Hear* talk in the street. There is much real poetry coming out of the mouths of people in the street. Many cliches, yes, but also vitality and colorful strengths.

4 Your poem does not need to tell your reader everything. A *little* mystery is fascinating. *Too much* is irritating.

5 Don't fall back on clichés—worn-out words and phrases. What worked for Wadsworth, Keats and Shelley is not likely to work for you.

6 Once in a while you may be able to redeem a cliché. Mix it up with unusual expressions. (*Warranted* unusual expressions!)

7 Don't use pretty words just because they're pretty. Don't use "thousand-dollar words" just because they are expensive. Your words, your phrases, your punctuation—all must prove they have specific jobs to do for you—jobs that drive you inexorably toward your resolution.

8 Permit a little freedom in your rhythms. Avoid consistent tightness, consistent strictness: Avoid music a la metronome: *back* forth, *back* forth. Here and there, allow yourself a few extra syllables. Allow yourself a little "unscheduled" irregularity. The unexpected looseness will enrich.

9 Write about what you know. Let yourself remember occurrences, incidents, experiences in your own life (and in the lives adjacent to yours) that made you feel happy, unhappy, angry, joyous, curious, frightened, apprehensive, suspicious, affectionate, meditative, precious, rejected, vital, sleepy-hearted.

10 Keep a journal. In it, write down anything that stirs you, impresses you. (see 9., above)

11 When you feel you are ready to write Your Poem, one way to proceed is as follows:

a. On a large sheet of paper write down everything you can think of or feel that concerns your subject—your theme—your "Inspiration." If lines and "beautiful" phrases begin to form themselves, get them down. But don't *force* them to "perfection": don't spend an hour polishing a line, in this your "first draft"— because you might forget *other* importances crowding your consciousness.

b. When you have your first draft down, begin to revise. Ask yourself, of each word before you—"Is this REALLY the word that says exactly what I want to say? Could another word say it better?" Revise your poem as many times as necessary. Revise your poem until you begin to see, on the page, yourself as you know yourself. Revise until you have secured for yourself a fresh, new poem, that says what you feel, think, suppose. Very exciting is the fact that during the writing of a poem you learn much about yourself that you had not before suspected.

12 In writing your poem, tell the truth as you know it. Tell *your* truth. Don't try to sugar it up. Don't force your poem to be nice or proper or normal or happy if it does not want to be. Remember that poetry is life distilled and that life is not always nice or proper or normal or happy or smooth or even-edged.

13 Do not be afraid to be found ahead of The Public's approbation. The Public's approbation is not always contemporary. It is often old-fashioned.

14 "Writer's block."
You're caught in the spell of your "career." For weeks, for months, you have been writing poem after poem after poem, merrily or soberly creating magic upon magic. Suddenly—"writer's block." You cannot think of any way to deliver the conception in your consciousness to paper. You are sure you will never write another poem. All the wonder is heavy wood.

Do not despair. Remember the following: no sickness continues in its exact state forever. The nature of life is change. In the grip of your sickness, "treat the symptoms." Put down your pen, pick up your books; read read read—for excitement's sake, for nourishment's sake; study, for the sake of enriching the *source* of your Nile. And *live:* go out into the world and cleanly involve yourself with the exhilarations of earth and air, involve yourself with people, young and old, new and known. Examine yourself: *you* are a vast world—travel in it, delve. Allow the necessary days to pass; *weeks* to pass; *months* to pass.

Finally, return to your pen and paper. Begin to record ideas, impressions, persuasions in your waiting journal. When your hand again seems easy, write a poem.
Expect to revise—as usual.
And expect future blocks!

15 Student's Question: "Does writing poems get easier as you go along?" No, writing poetry never gets "easier." And why and how SHOULD it get "easier"?
Each poem is a kingdom in, to, of itself. Achieving Poem One does not guarantee achievement of Poem Two or Ten or Twelve Hundred.

16 A Visit to an Elementary School.
Subject: Reading and Writing Poetry.
A popular question: What is poetry? Poetry, I answer frequently, is what poets write. And a poet is a person who distils experience, then crystallizes. The crystals may then be held familiarly in the hand. Prose endeavors to say very much about a thing; Poetry is at pains to select—poetry selects with agonized care. Prose is survey; poetry is siren. Poetry is beauty, or music, or condensed thought—or all of these at once—drawn from or spirited from, or molded out of, human experience.

I asked my daughter, for eight years a magnificent teacher and now the founder-director of Anchor Arts Organization for Children. "What do you think poetry is?" A little girl of thirteen then, she answered: "I think that poetry is that quality which enables us to see clearly light, joy, gaiety, sorrow, sadness. It is that quality which we need most in the world, because without it we would not really know what the world is." (February 9, 1965; at home.)

I have brought you some poems.
I hope you like poetry.

Please don't hate it just because your teachers have made you memorize it. Poetry *really is* life. It is life, sifted through a strainer. It is life distilled. Young poets, when you write a poem, remember that every word in it must work, must do a specific job. Tolerate no lazy words. Tolerate no words stuck in *only* for prettiness' sake. Remember, also, that you don't HAVE to rhyme. Indeed, the attempt to rhyme is often crippling, limiting, inhibiting. (On the other hand, of course, rhyme can sometimes be an assistant to the imagination, an idea-*extender*. If you do insist on rhyming, try unusual rhymes. Avoid such obvious rhymes as cat-rat, day-gray, song-long, love-above, star-far, June-moon, June-tune.) Choose language fresh, immediate, evocative.

17 Stimulating an affection for poetry in schools:

 a. Students should not be forced to memorize poetry. Remembering poetry they want to remember—that's one thing. But forced memorizing tends to freeze a poem in at the level it was first met. What you thought of it then you will, perhaps, *always* think of it. But that is not right, because a poem should mean different things to you, for you, at different times in your life. Its meanings should be free to shift or grow, even as yourself.

 b. Students should be encouraged to read poetry widely. And they should be encouraged to read about poetry. As a strong preparatory spur, they might be given Elizabeth Drew's *Poetry: A Modern Guide to Its Understanding* and *Enjoyment*. They might be given Edmund Wilson's *Axel's Castle,* studies in symbolist poetry. Black poets will profit from Stephen Henderson's *Understanding the New Black Poetry,* Eugene Redmond's *Drumvoices,* Don L. Lee's {Haki R. Madhubuti} *Dynamite Voices,* and *A Capsule Course in Black Poetry Writing* (Randall, Brooks, Madhubuti, Kgositsile.) Hispanic aids: look for the political and the autobiographical in contemporary Hispanic writing. You should study Hispanic prose as well a the vibrant poetry. Discover the prose as well the vibrant poetry. Discover the prose of Carlos Fuentes. Read Piri Thomas' *Down These Mean Streets.* Investigate the current Latino "Beer Boom" writing (called that to suggest fluent and ready talking and the shedding of masks.) Other references: the poetry of Chicagoan Sandra Cisneros: Octavio Paz—the *Bow and the Lyre* (Texas University Press) and *Alternating Current* (Compass Press).

c. Students should be encouraged to buy poetry recordings. The Caedmon series of verse read by the poets themselves is exciting, inclusive. (I, too, have a record in this series, entitled *Gwendolyn Brooks Reads Her Poetry.*)

18 Young people, in much great poetry you will hear the community *speaking*. And the community often speaks in terms of poetry. Earlier here, I suggested that you listen to voices in the street, that very often it is *poetry* you will be hearing. Raw, perhaps (although often as cooked as you'd want)—but the nuances, the toning, the fire will be there for a willing ear to credit.

The community, incidentally, often converses in iambic pentameter:
I wish that I could get away today.
The little leaves are coming out again.
Johnny, I love you. Let me take your hand.
I think you need salvation right away.
I ate an apple just the other day.
Beyond the magic there is life after death.
The lemonade is bitter. Sugar, please.

19 Human sources of poetry: the items of the poet's essential interior and the reactions of those items to whatever he or she encounters in the world.

20 Feel free to talk on your paper about anything, not just flowers and trees and springtime. Write about what you see on television and your *honest* response to it, write about what you see in the street, what you see in the newspapers. Write about church, basketball and football, swimming, picnics, discos, horses, ants, rock music, hymns, the kitchen stove, coffee, tea, war, pancakes, milk shakes, Zimbabwe, love and hate, marbles, kites, blood, grape jelly, riots, Paris gowns and the fact that you do not have any, blue jeans, space, daisies and dandelions, orchids and the fact that you do not want any (maybe you do), teenagers, "old" people (who are merely people who happen to have been around a long time and whom you're going to look like sooner than think), hospitals, prisons, Sunkist oranges, McDonald's hamburgers, gardens, garbage cans, bicycles, Toyotas, sickness, health, your roots, grasshoppers, détente, an old tattered living room rug, Malcolm X, Mao, mice, mountains and mercy. Jimmy Carter, The Ayatollah Khomeini. About all or any of these subjects write what you REALLY think and feel. What YOU think. What YOU feel.

21   Some "salvations" for poetry; some suggestions toward a wider interest in poetry:—
large print!
Better poetry SAYING
I think, also, that we'll have more success with the often bewildered "public" if we allow the clothes of a poem to grow right out of its bones. (Don't *impose* decoration.)

22   You do not have to use punctuation in your poem. Many good poems contain no punctuation at all. But if you use it, you must be sure that it isn't lazy. It must *labor* toward your *ultimacy*.

23   What is Black poetry? Black poetry is poetry written by Blacks, about Blacks, to Blacks. Black poetry features urgencies of Black unity, Black churning, Black exhilaration, Black caring and curing.

Note: much contemporary Black poetry features "The Dozens"—a play on language and feelings, geared to smart, to sting, to quicken—but not to lay low, not too flatten: because the opponent, the "victim", the partner, must be left equipped for re-challenge.

24   Is a poetry workshop necessary for everyone who wants to write poetry? One justification for a writing workshop is its efficiency in enabling you to write readily and on a regular basis. When you are young, the closeness of other people, all trying together to achieve, all sometimes failing, all sometimes triumphing, can be gratifying. As you grow older you will find that you need less togetherness, that it is easier for you, without reliance on others, to make what is in you clear to yourself and accessible, enjoyable, *relevant* to your readers.

25   About readers. Now and again I meet a poet who assures me *"I write for myself, not for other people."* What about "writing for self," as opposed to writing for self and *others*? Answer: If you show your work *only* to yourself, *always*, you are one of the few individuals truly self-concerned and only self-concerned, writing for self alone. It is a thin business, with cold rewards.

26   Art hurts. Art urges voyages.

27   We live with poetic symbol.
     Any flag is a piece of poetry. It beautifully, simply, and in condensed fashion shouts out a great many things that it would take most of us a long time to put into words.

28   Of "success": first, there must be a deal of Wanting. You're going to get very little in this life without the *first* step of some powerful Wanting.

29　It is not necessary for you to carry the rules of meter, form, scansion in your head. I want you to get an excellent text—Elizabeth Drew's *Poetry: A Modern Guide to Its Understanding and Enjoyment,* published by Delta (paperback). I've mentioned it earlier in this Primer, and I include it in a list of recommendations at the back. This book excuses you for not carrying meters, forms, scansion in your head: it isolates such information in an appendix.

30　Poetry HAS a future! You MAY initiate new forms. You MAY create. You do NOT have to consider that "everything has been done." You do NOT have to write sonnets, villanelles, heroic couplets, haiku, tanka, simply because centuries of poets have written such. Dare to invent something. Understand that *some*body invented the sonnet. Understand: the day before the sonnet was invented there *was* no sonnet.

31　As often as you have the opportunity, go to poetry readings and poetry festivals.

32　Television:
Study the literary programs on your educational television station. Study the plays. Shakespeare's plays. Other plays, new and old. Products of all available cultures. And, because your springs must be fed variously, study "Nova," study the National Geographic television features. Do not ignore programs that offer you history, science, biography.

33　Frequent question—Does poetry make anything happen? Poetry has been known to alter opinion. From altered opinion "happenings" evolve.

EDITORS' NOTE: Tip #29 refers to a list of recommendations prepared by Gwendolyn Brooks. We chose to leave it out because all of those suggestions are mentioned throughout Young Poet's Primer. An updated list of recommendations is provided by Quraysh Ali Lansana in A Study Guide for SEASONS A Gwendolyn Brooks Experience.

Credits

A STREET IN BRONZEVILLE
Harper & Brothers, 1945
A Song in the Front Yard
When You Have Forgotten
    Sunday
Beverly Hills, Chicago
my dreams, my works, must
    wait till after hell
Kitchenette Building
of De Witt Williams on His
    Way to Lincoln Cemetery

ANNIE ALLEN
Harper & Brothers, 1949
Old Laughter
the children of the poor (2)
Truth (IX)
The Womanhood (II)

MAUD MARTHA
Harper & Brothers, 1953/
Third World Press, 1992
Home
Maud Martha Spares the Mouse
Clement Lewy

BRONZEVILLE BOYS AND
GIRLS
Harper & Brothers, 1956
Cynthia in the Snow

THE BEAN EATERS
Harper, 1960
The Bean Eaters
Old People Working
    (garden, car)
A Sunset of the City
The Crazy Woman
Pete at the Zoo
Big Bessie Throws Her Son into
    the Street
To Be In Love
We Real Cool
Chicago Defender Sends A Man
    to Little Rock

IN THE MECCA
Harper & Row, 1968
Malcolm X
Sermon On the Warpland
Blackstone Rangers: As Seen By
    Disciplines

RIOT
Broadside Press, 1969
An Aspect of Love Alive in the
    Ice and Fire

ALONENESS
Broadside Press, 1971
Poem of the same name

YOUNG POET'S PRIMER
Brooks Press, 1971
*A collection of writing tips by the
    same name*

FAMILY PICTURES
Broadside Press, 1971
The Life of Lincoln West
Young Heroes II
    (To Don at Salaam)
Paul Robeson
Speech to the Young Speech to
    the Progress-Toward

BECKONINGS
Broadside Press, 1975
The Boy Died in My Alley
When Handed A Lemon, Make
    Lemonade

PRIMER FOR BLACKS
Brooks Press, 1981
To Those Of My Sisters Who
    Kept Their Naturals

TO DISEMBARK
Third World Press 1981
To Black Women

THE NEAR-
JOHANNESBURG BOY
Third World Press 1987
Infirm
The Near-Johannesburg Boy
To The Young Who Want To
    Die

GOTTSCHALK AND THE
GRAND TARANTELLE
The David Company, 1989
Thinking of Elizabeth Steinberg

CHILDREN COMING HOME
The David Company, 1991
Song: White Powder
Kojo: I Am A Black
Uncle Seagram
To Be Grown Up

REPORT FROM PART TWO
Third World Press 1996
Parents:
*(A longer version of
this piece appears in
Report From Part One)*

IN MONTGOMERY
...and Other Poems
Third World Press, 2003
A Girl Behind the Scenes
Jane Addams
Patrick Bouie of Cabrini-Green
Art
An Old Black Woman,
    Homeless, And Indistinct
Old Woman Rap
Martin Luther King Jr.
Black Love
Aurora *(Originally printed as a
    broadside. Broadside Press,
    1972)*

PREVIOUSLY
UNPUBLISHED WORKS
Forgive & Forget *(referenced
in Report From Part One)*
Old

137